JAN 17

D1212274

Awful, Disgusting Parasites

BEDBUGS

MARGARET MINCKS

BLACK
RABBIT
BOOKS

BOLT

Bolt is published by Black Rabbit Books
P.O. Box 3263, Mankato, Minnesota, 56002.
www.blackrabbitbooks.com
Copyright © 2017 Black Rabbit Books

Design and Production by Brad Norr and
Michael Sellner
Photo Research by Rhonda Milbrett

Library of Congress Control Number: 2015954681

HC ISBN: 978-1-68072-006-8   PB ISBN: 978-1-68072-270-3

Printed in the United States at CG Book Printers,
North Mankato, Minnesota, 56003. PO #1792 4/16

Web addresses included in this book were working and appropriate
at the time of publication. The publisher is not responsible for broken
or changed links.

Image Credits

Corbis: Andrew Wallace/ZUMA
Press, 23; David Scharf, Cover; David
Spears FRPS FRMS, 17; Dennis Kunkel Mi-
croscopy, Inc./Visuals Unlimited, 24; Dr. Robert
Calentine/Visuals Unlimited, 21; Ingo Arndt/Min-
den Pictures, 3, 32; Piotr Naskrecki/Minden Pictures,
6–7; © Science Picture Co., 8; Visuals Unlimited, 12;
Dreamstime: © Margaret M Stewart, 24; © MorganOliver,
22–23; iStock: SolomonPhotos, 11; James Kalisch, UNL
Dept of Entomology, 26; Shutterstock: 3drenderings, 31;
Crystal Eye Studio, 14–15; Hein Nouwens, 29; Joao Luiz
Lima, 24; lantapix, 18–19; Marco Uliana, 16, 20–21,
22; Morphart Creation, 18–19; smuay, 27; Wikimedia:
Jacopo Werther, 1, 4–5, 14–15 (background); Piotr
Naskrecki, 8
Every effort has been made to contact copyright
holders for material reproduced in this book.
Any omissions will be rectified in subse-
quent printings if notice is given
to the publisher.

Contents

CHAPTER 1

Meet the

When the sun is up, bedbugs stay hidden. They camp out in beds and walls. But at night, they crawl out for a snack. What's on the menu? Blood!

Bedbugs are **parasites**. They live and feed on humans and other animals. They are only about the size of apple seeds. Their small size makes them hard to find.

5

BEDBUG BODY PARTS

ANTENNAE

HEAD

THORAX

ABDOMEN

LEGS

Bedbugs sometimes poop on their victims after eating.

Hungry Hitchhikers

Bedbugs can't fly or jump. Instead, they crawl. Sometimes they tag along in **luggage**. They also catch rides on pets and clothing.

All that travel makes bedbugs hungry. First, they crawl on a human or other animal. Then they bite. When bedbugs bite, their spit gets into their victims. Bedbug spit has a special ingredient that **numbs** the skin. The victims don't feel a thing!

CHAPTER 2

A Bedbug's Life

Bedbugs have three life stages. They start life as eggs. Then they grow into **nymphs** and then into adults.

A female bedbug can lay five eggs each day. Females lay eggs in hidden places, such as folds in bed sheets. Each egg is smaller than a pinhead.

The Days of Their Lives

Bedbugs eat every **3-7 days.**

It takes up to **14 days** for a bedbug bite to show.

Bedbugs live **180-365 days.**

days 0   50

From Nymphs to Adults

Bedbug eggs hatch in six to 17 days. These young bugs are called nymphs. They look like small adult bedbugs.

As nymphs grow, they shed their **exoskeletons** five times. Bedbug nymphs become adults in less than eight weeks.

100   150   200   250   300   350   400

BEDBUG LIFE CYCLE

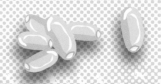

EGG

ADULT

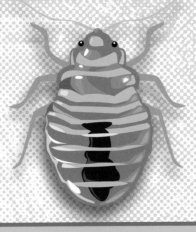

5TH STAGE

1ST STAGE
NYMPH

2ND STAGE

3RD STAGE

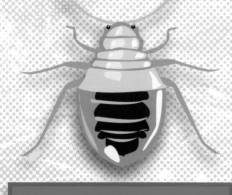

4TH STAGE

15

CHAPTER 3

Attack
of the Bedbugs

Bedbugs live all over the world. They are most often found where people sleep. Hotels, ships, and trains are hot spots for bedbugs.

Bedbugs like big cities. In 2010, New York City had a bedbug panic. People found bedbugs in hotels, theaters, and subways. Even the Empire State Building had the pests.

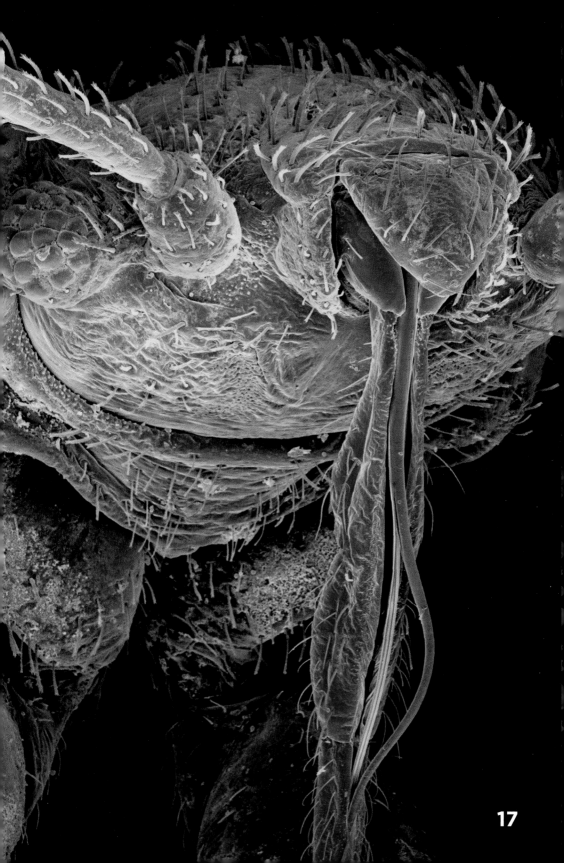

17

BEDBUGS RANGE MAP

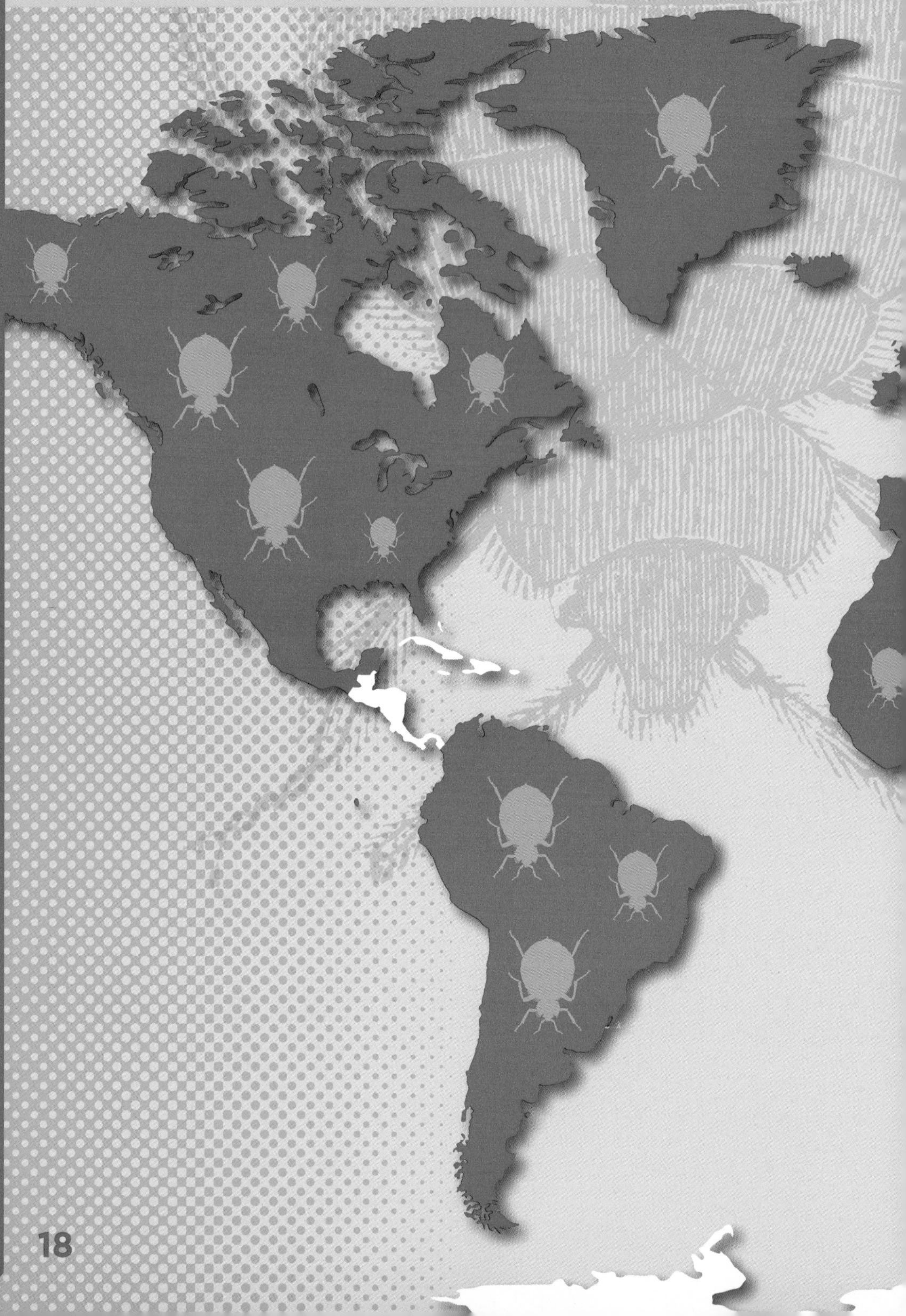

CHAPTER 4

Don't Let the

Bite!

Bedbug bites can be painless. They may look like mosquito bites. Bedbugs usually bite on the face, neck, hands, and arms. Sometimes bites cause itching or big bumps.

Bedbugs by the
Numbers

0.25 INCH (.6 CM)

average length of a bedbug

13,742
bedbug complaints in New York City in 2010

5 TO 15 MINUTES
time it takes for a bedbug to fill with blood

100 FEET
(30 M)
distance a bedbug will travel for a meal

122°F (50°C)
highest known temperature at which a bedbug can survive

Hard to Stop

Bedbugs are tiny and only come out at night. This makes them hard to catch. Professional **exterminators** use **pesticides** to kill bedbugs. They also use heat, cold, and traps.

Some dogs are trained to sniff out bedbugs.

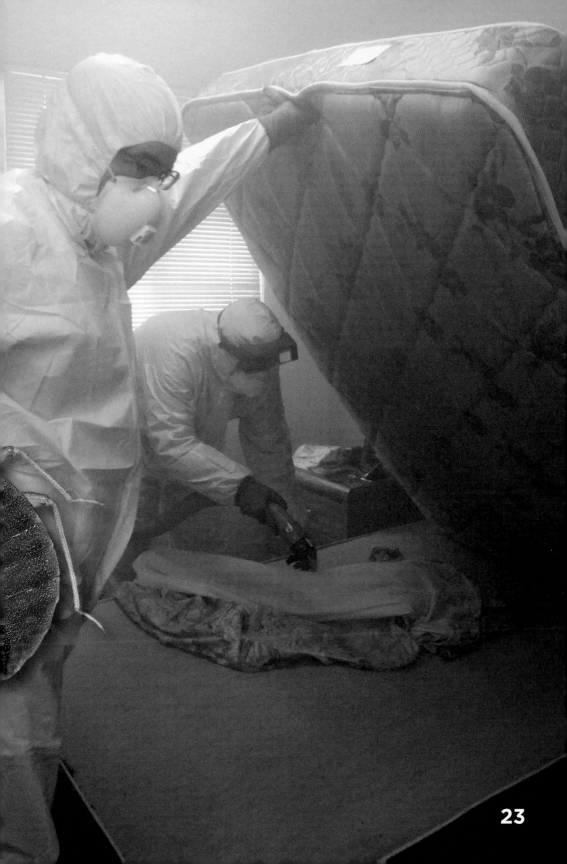

exoskeletons on sheets and mattresses

rust-colored blood spots on sheets and mattresses

Bedbug Prevention

It's hard to stop bedbugs. But there are some ways to prevent getting them. If staying in a hotel, keep bags off the floor. Make sure to wash clothes after a trip. At home, keep living spaces neat. Don't give bedbugs a place to hide.

dead bugs in the folds of sheets and mattresses

SIGNS OF BEDBUGS

a sweet, musty scent

Sleep Tight

Bedbugs are parasites that travel around. They suck people's blood. But luckily, they don't spread diseases. Just stay alert for these pests when traveling. Then sleep tight!

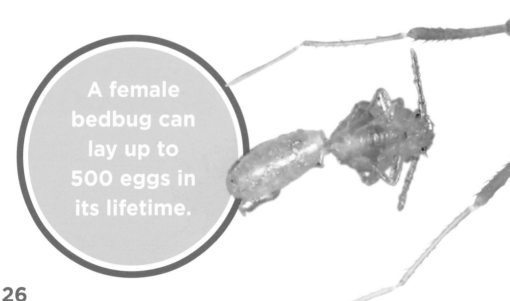

A female bedbug can lay up to 500 eggs in its lifetime.

Take Two  Bedbugs, and Call Me in the Morning

Ancient Romans made medicines using bedbugs. They thought these medicines could cure snakebites, ear infections, and other illnesses.

Imagine you're in ancient Rome, suffering from a painful snakebite. Would you snack on bedbugs to feel better?

exoskeleton (ek-so-SKE-le-ten)—the hard, protective cover on the outside of an insect's body

exterminator (ex-TUR-min-ay-tuhr)—a person who kills bugs and other pests

luggage (LUG-ej)—the bags or suitcases used when traveling

numb (NUM)—unable to feel a part of the body

nymph (NIMPF)—a young insect that has almost the same form as the adult

parasite (PAR-uh-syt)—a plant or animal that lives in or on another plant or animal and gets its food or protection from it

pesticide (PES-tuh-syd)—a chemical used to kill pests

BOOKS

Gleason, Carrie. *Feasting Bedbugs, Mites, and Ticks.* Creepy Crawlies. New York: Crabtree Pub., 2011.

Jeffries, Joyce. *Bedbugs.* Freaky Freeloaders. New York: PowerKids Press, 2015.

Morey, Allan. *Insects.* Animal Kingdom. Mankato, MN: Amicus High Interest, 2015.

WEBSITES

Bedbugs
www.kidshealth.org/parent/infections/parasitic/bedbugs.html

Bed Bugs
www.pestworldforkids.org/pest-guide/bed-bugs/

Bed Bugs
video.nationalgeographic.com/video/bedbugs